PUFFI[N]

ALL
THE COMPLETE,

All Saints are Shaznay Lewis, Melanie Blatt and sisters Nicole and Natalie Appleton – all extremely talented, drop-dead gorgeous Londoners in their early twenties. But they are no overnight sensation. They have spent five long, hard years slogging away to break into the charts. But now their wildest dreams have come true and the hard work has paid off. All Saints are on their way to becoming one of the biggest bands in the world.

Another book by Jeremy Case

HERE'S HANSON

Jeremy Case

All Saints

THE COMPLETE, UNOFFICIAL STORY

PUFFIN BOOKS

PUFFIN BOOKS

Published by the Penguin Group
Penguin Books Ltd, 27 Wrights Lane, London W8 5TZ, England
Penguin Putnam Inc., 375 Hudson Street, New York, New York 10014, USA
Penguin Books Australia Ltd, Ringwood, Victoria, Australia
Penguin Books Canada Ltd, 10 Alcorn Avenue, Toronto, Ontario, Canada M4V 3B2
Penguin Books (NZ) Ltd, Cnr Rosedale and Airborne Roads, Albany, Auckland,
New Zealand

Penguin Books Ltd, Registered Offices: Harmondsworth, Middlesex, England

First published 1998
1 3 5 7 9 10 8 6 4 2

Copyright © Jeremy Case, 1998
All rights reserved

The moral right of the author has been asserted

Set in 14/17 Bembo

Made and printed in England by Clays Ltd, St Ives plc

Except in the United States of America, this book is sold subject to the condition that
it shall not, by way of trade or otherwise, be lent, re-sold, hired out, or otherwise
circulated without the publisher's prior consent in any form of binding or cover other
than that in which it is published and without a similar condition including
this condition being imposed on the subsequent purchaser

British Library Cataloguing in Publication Data
A CIP catalogue record for this book is available from the British Library

ISBN 0–141–30292–5

Contents

1 All Saints' Day   1
2 Let's Get Started   8
3 What's the Big Deal?   16
4 Tricky Nicky   24
5 Nat's Show Business   34
6 Simply Shaz   44
7 Heaven and Mel   52
8 Songs in the Key of Life   62
9 Who Wears the Trousers?   69
10 Saints in Heaven   74
11 What's in Store?   85

CHAPTER ONE

All Saints' Day

In the race to grab the coveted Christmas number-one spot in December '97, one record emerged from the pile that was so good that it was 'Never Ever' going to be forgotten. It proved its worth by hanging around the notoriously fickle pop charts for nine long weeks, selling 770,000 copies in total *before* finally reaching number one in January 1998. That's more than any other single in chart history.

That record of course was All Saints' massive single, 'Never Ever'. In all it remained in the top ten for over three months, a feat only equalled at the time by Robbie Williams' 'Angels'. The group went on to perform the song live on *TOTP* a staggering ten times.

The four members of All Saints – Shaznay Lewis, Melanie Blatt, and sisters Nicole and Natalie

Appleton are all extremely talented, drop-dead gorgeous Londoners in their early twenties. But they are no overnight sensation. They had spent five long, hard years slogging away to bag that precious number-one spot, at times being so poor that they only had one Pot Noodle to share between them. Suddenly all their wildest dreams had come true. 'We thought "Never Ever" would do well, but we had no idea how well,' admits Shaz.

Their debut single, 'I Know Where It's At', had also taken the charts by storm, reaching number four in the UK and, showing that All Saints weren't just a British phenomenon, it made number thirty-two in America and the top five as far away as New Zealand, and number one in Japan. A few months later, 'Never Ever' would reach the top twenty in Denmark and Norway and the top five in Ireland, Poland and the Netherlands, proving that there was no limit to the scale of their success.

Back home, All Saints had to postpone the release of their third single, 'Under the Bridge/Lady Marmalade', three times because 'Never Ever' was still disappearing off record-shop shelves at a fantastic rate. But when it was finally released, it too went straight in at number one. The girls were becoming a permanent fixture at the top of the charts. Meanwhile, their self-titled album has sold 2.4 million copies and rising throughout the world. Not bad for a band that nobody had even heard of a year ago!

Before they knew it, All Saints were featured in every teen magazine going, gracing the covers of *Smash Hits*, *Live & Kicking*, *Big* and *TOTP Magazine*, all at the same time. They soon discovered that their fans weren't only teenagers but included people of all ages and backgrounds. These girls weren't just relying on their looks and personalities (although they had bags of both), they could write killer tunes that were loved by people from all walks of life. Their crossover appeal was proven when Mark Sutherland, editor of serious music paper *Melody Maker* (which normally only covers indie bands like The Verve and Oasis), chose 'Never Ever' as his favourite single of 1997. 'Everyone else was talking about perfect pop. All Saints just went out and made some,' he wrote.

All Saints could even boast royal approval. Princes William and Harry loved 'Never Ever' and asked for pictures of the girls to be sent to them. So the band supplied Buckingham Palace with a bumper pack of signed photos and personal messages. And when William couldn't join Harry and his father for tea with the Spice Girls, he was rumoured to have said he wasn't too bothered because he preferred All Saints anyway!

The girls proved beyond doubt that they were here to stay when they walked off with a bunch of music industry prizes early in 1998. They won Best Newcomer at the Music of Black Origin awards, and performed live alongside the likes of queen of swing Mary J Blige and the massive Blackstreet.

Then in February '98, they won two coveted Brit awards – Best Video for 'Never Ever', voted by viewers of the Box satellite TV station and Best Single for 'Never Ever', voted by the public. They were just pipped for a third award – Best Newcomer – by the Stereophonics. To celebrate they gave a stunning live performance of 'Never Ever', backed by a gospel choir and full orchestra.

For the four Londoners it was an especially sweet triumph. The girls had bagged the very same two awards that had been won twelve months previously by that other legendary all-female group – the Spice Girls.

All Saints had finally escaped from the shadow of the Spices. They had been asked about the Fab

Five in every interview they'd ever done and had been compared, often unfavourably, to the group in every article ever printed. When they were struggling to get a record deal, their bosses had tried to persuade them to be more like the Spice Girls. And then, when they finally made it into the charts, they were accused of jumping on the bandwagon, of merely riding on the back of the 'Girl Power' phenomenon.

All this despite the fact that All Saints had been around two or three years longer. Neither was their music particularly similar. All Saints had more in common with American female soul and R & B acts like En Vogue, TLC and Janet Jackson, as opposed to the pure bubblegum pop of the Spice Girls.

Journalists made up a 'Spice Girls v All Saints' battle, comparing it to other great pop rivalries of the past, such as The Beatles vs the Rolling Stones, Oasis vs Blur and Take That vs East 17. And they even tried to think up Spice-style nicknames for the Saints, such as Shy Saint for Shaz and Mouthy Saint for Mel. But, unsurprisingly, these never caught on, because while the Spice Girls have always emphasized the different personalities in their group, All Saints are first and foremost a band, a group of girls with a shared love of music and a common dream. They are so much of a unit that the papers keep getting them mixed up, especially the Appleton sisters.

'Respect to the Spice Girls for what they're doing,' says Shaz. 'They make a lot of people happy. But our music's different. We're a real group. We're not manufactured. Spice is a phenomenon and it can't happen again for a long time.' And she insists that there are no hard feelings (although the Saints have been known to come out with the occasional outburst): 'Everyone goes round saying we hate them, but we don't. We admire them, because they've done what they wanted to do. We're totally different and that's that.'

The same message comes from the Spice Girls, who were seen singing along backstage as All Saints performed 'Never Ever' at the Brits. 'All we want to do is to have lots of beers with All Saints and have a laugh,' says Mel C. 'We love their music and we're really glad they're doing so well.'

Editor of *Smash Hits*, Gavin Reeves, believes that soon the debate will be forgotten. 'People will stop comparing them once they establish themselves,' he says. 'The quality of the girls' voices is exceptional, outstanding. They are sexier and more streetwise.'

If you look beneath the surface, the differences between the two bands become more obvious than the similarities. The Spice Girls are loud and showy. All Saints are subdued, sophisticated and totally dedicated to music – tellingly they even have pop stars for boyfriends. Many people believe that they will be around for far, far longer. And in a way, All Saints are much more about Girl Power than the Spice Girls themselves. Traditionally all-female groups have always had a man behind the scenes pulling the strings, but All Saints have done it all themselves, the hard way. They have stuck to their guns, refused to compromise and now their songs have touched millions of music fans throughout the world, regardless of sex, age or nationality. 'We're into People Power,' says Nat. 'Whoever you are, whichever sex, just go for it.'

All Saints' story is an inspiration for anyone who has a dream and is prepared to make as many sacrifices as are necessary along the way to fulfil it. If you put your mind to something there is nothing to stop you achieving your goal. This is how All Saints did just that.

CHAPTER TWO

Let's Get Started

All Saints didn't answer a newspaper advert like many of today's teenage sensations. On the contrary, their story involves hard work, sweat, tears and a never-failing dedication. They always knew they wanted to be musicians, but had to struggle for years on peanuts to realize their dream.

Their story begins in a recording studio in a street called All Saints Road in Notting Hill, London. It was here that the two original members of the band, Melanie and Shaznay, bumped into each other aged sixteen and became friends.

Shaz had been entering singing contests since she was thirteen. 'I had always sung at school, wrote little poems and rapped for my friends,' she says. 'Even if I'd ended up working in a shop, I would have still been singing on the side.' And when she wasn't driving her parents mad by sneaking out to go to rap gigs and watch bands, she'd be in her bedroom, pretending to be a DJ. 'I'd introduce a record and then I'd have to be that record, so I taped myself singing everything from Madonna to Whitney Houston,' she recalls. Eventually she got work recording with other artists, such as Ben from former eighties' boy band Curiosity Killed The Cat, who she met at a party. But even that nearly didn't happen – Shaz was too shy to talk to him and her friends had to introduce them. He suggested they went to a studio straight away and Shaz ended up jamming with him and a load of professional musicians almost all night.

Mel was just as keen to be in a band. 'I'd sit on the studio couch and listen to everything that was going on,' she says. 'I used to make tea. I wasn't being paid. Eventually they let me sing backing vocals for people. That's all I did for two years.'

Inevitably the two bumped into each other and soon found they had a great deal in common, even if there were some nerves at first. 'I remember being terrified of Shaznay when I first saw her,' says Mel. 'I didn't have any girlfriends my age at the time and when she walked in with her mates I thought, "God, she's so pretty." I was really intimidated.' Luckily, Shaz wasn't so timid ('I thought Mel looked really girly, quiet and innocent,' she says) and the two hit it off straight away.

'Shaznay and I were on the same wavelength,' explains Mel. 'We did loads of session work but we weren't really going anywhere, so we formed a band.' And so they got together with another girl at the studio, seventeen-year-old Simone Rainford, and All Saints (Mark One) was born. Working out what to call themselves wasn't easy though. 'One of the names was Spice, but we didn't think it was good enough,' admits Simone. Other names bandied around included Slinky and Shifty. But in the end they called themselves All Saints 1.9.7.5. after the recording studio and the year of their births.

At first, everything went brilliantly. The trio were snapped up almost immediately by a small label called ZTT in 1993 and gave their first live performance at London's Notting Hill Carnival the following year. But problems soon began to set in as the girls couldn't decide what kind of music they wanted to make. 'All we were asked to do was other people's songs,' moans Mel. Their first single, a cover of old soul song, 'Silver Shadow', released in 1994, was a resounding failure.

Shaz and, in particular, Mel, weren't getting on too well with Simone either. 'We were only seventeen or eighteen at the time, so we were really naive and hardly knew each other when we signed the deal,' says Shaz. 'Simone needed to be a solo artist. I think she only decided to join for the sake of a deal, not because she thought we all got on well together.' After a year, in the summer of 1995, the musical differences and bust-ups became too much and Simone left.

And while Mel and Shaz went on to unimagined global success, Simone is still struggling to get her solo career off the ground. 'I wasn't surprised when All Saints made it big,' she admits. 'I just wish things had turned out differently. Now I'd be making millions too. I'm going to try my hardest to make it big on my own. But I haven't got any regrets. Not really.'

Back then, life was really tough for Shaz and Mel too. 'We were broke when we started,' says Shaz. 'We lived off fritters from a West Indian café where Mel had a tab, which is still outstanding. We used to say, "We'll pay you back because we're going to be big one day." It's taken five years.'

They released a second single called 'If You Wanna Party (I Found Lovin')', another cover, on

25 September 1995, but it flopped too. (If you can find a copy of either of these singles now, you could sell them for a fortune!) Meanwhile, the girls were working on their own original sound, but were struggling to mix their British and American influences.

The only highlight of their two years at ZTT was playing the *Smash Hits* tour with Boyzone, Peter Andre and the Backstreet Boys in November '95. 'That was the best thing ever,' remembers Shaz, although the girls were left completely to themselves to prepare for their act. 'I went round to Mel's house to learn a dance routine and a friend of mine sat on the bed and held up a mirror so that we could see what we looked like while we practised.'

The tour gave the duo an early taste of stardom, but off stage everybody seemed to ignore them. 'There was one day when everyone else was doing TV appearances or interviews and we were sitting in the hotel, doing nothing,' remembers Shaz. 'It wasn't like our music wasn't good enough, either – we'd already recorded a version of "I Know Where It's At" – and everyone we played it to loved it. It made us think, "Oh man, this isn't good."'

ZTT must have thought so too because two

months later they were dropped from the label. But far from getting down and chucking it all in, the teenagers saw it as a chance to finally work on their own material. 'The *Smash Hits* tour made us determined to carry on and do our own thing,' says Shaz.

It wasn't easy. The girls were completely broke and had to take on odd jobs and rely on favours. 'I don't know how Mel and I survived,' Shaz grimaces. 'I even temped over Christmas, at Top Man, and it was a nightmare. It lasted about two weeks. Then I worked in a men's clothes shop for three weeks, as a favour for a friend.' Luckily, the girls earned free studio time in exchange for their singing work, though if it hadn't been for the support of their families and friends, it's hard to see how they could have kept going.

But not everyone was out to help them. In their early days in the music business, the girls were inexperienced and it sometimes showed. 'For years we'd meet people in the studio who'd promise us a deal and it would never actually happen. We were still babies. All we knew back then was that we loved making music. Outside of that, we didn't have a clue,' says Shaz.

On the plus side, their songwriting was

improving all the time. And soon they found they needed more voices to add harmony to Shaz's soulful melodies. Despite auditioning what seemed like an endless list of hopefuls, it wasn't until they ran into Nicole and Natalie Appleton that Shaz and Mel realized they were on to something.

Nic and Nat had attended the same drama school as Mel many years before, and that seemed to be something of a lucky charm. The list of past pupils is astonishing and includes Spice Girl Emma Bunton, *EastEnder* Daniella Westbrook (Sam Butcher), actress Samantha Janus and *Big Breakfast* presenter Denise Van Outen. At school Nic and Mel became inseparable. But then Mel's family had moved to France and the Appletons went to New York. 'I never stopped thinking about her,' says Nic. 'I knew we would meet up again. When we ran into each other, it was as though we had never been apart.'

Mel didn't know her best friend had returned to London until her dad, a taxi driver at the time, bumped into Nic at a TGI Friday restaurant in May '96. 'It was fate,' says Mel. But she was too embarrassed to ask her mate to join the band so it was left to the normally shy Shaz to pop the question. 'We gave her the low-down on everything and played her some demos, which she loved,' she says. 'She sang to me in the bathroom of a restaurant and we knew right away she'd be perfect. I was like, "Cool! She can join!" And that was that.'

Nic didn't have to think twice. 'I'd been doing odd jobs like waitressing, working on a hot-dog stand, a lifeguard. I had nothing to lose.'

Nat was a different story. She was just as enthusiastic about All Saints as her younger sister, but because she was two years older and more business-minded, at first she thought about becoming their manager. 'Then one day, it just clicked,' says Shaz. 'Nat had so much energy and was so excited about getting us a deal, it seemed only natural that she should be a part of it.' After a little persuasion, Nat took the plunge and the line-up was complete. In Shaz's words, 'When Nat joined, it was like the missing piece of the puzzle.'

Suddenly it all clicked. The Appleton sisters' American influence gave an extra edge to All Saints' transatlantic sound, while Nic's energy and enthusiasm and Nat's maturity blended perfectly with Mel's mad outbursts and Shaz's quiet genius. All Saints were ready to take on the world.

CHAPTER THREE

What's the Big Deal?

The line-up may have been sorted, but the four girls were going nowhere unless they could land another record deal – and the new-look All Saints were going to have to make many sacrifices to get to the top. 'We were on the dole and just dedicated our lives to hanging around studios, sharing one Pot Noodle between us and recording when we could,' says Mel, who admits she used to cry herself to sleep at night worrying about the band.

And even though All Saints knew they had written songs that could easily compete with anything on *TOTP*, they couldn't understand why they still didn't have two pennies to rub together. In fact, things got so bad that they decided to split with their manager, Paul Hallett, and try their luck with someone else. The move helped their career, but it cost them later on, as in early 1998 they were legally forced to pay him £500,000 for his part in their rise to fame.

It was the outgoing, confident Nic who found them a new manager, which quickly led to a deal. She spotted a guy from the music business called John Benson in a nightclub and marched up to tell him that All Saints were the best thing since sliced bread and that he would be a prize idiot if he didn't agree to become their manager. Luckily, Benson did agree with her. He quickly realized the four girls had the ability to make it. 'It had to be polished,' he says. 'But I know what's good.'

Unfortunately, All Saints' timing was all wrong and they kept finding they were being compared unfavourably with other girl bands. Originally people said they were too similar to Eternal and then of course the Spice Girls exploded on to the scene in the summer of 1996. Suddenly every label wanted their own copycat version. But All Saints stuck to their guns. 'We couldn't change and be who they wanted us to be, it wouldn't have lasted,' says Nat.

'We decided to wait to find a label that was interested in our music and didn't want to change us. That's real girl power,' adds Shaz.

In reality, the waiting took its toll – the girls were getting fed up with the comparisons. Mel says it's amazing that they didn't just pack it all in and give up. She had to borrow money from people all over west London and is still bitter about their experiences: 'People see four young girls and think they can manipulate us. Who wants to be told how to look, how to wear your make-up and what to say?'

All Saints were brave enough to turn down three offers from other labels, one from mega-famous Sony, because of these very reasons. 'None of them cared about the songs,' says Nat. 'They would demand that we start showing "our feminine side". We're not boys. We can dress like elegant women and we love to look good, but when we do our music, we want to be comfortable.'

Fortunately for All Saints' fans all over the world, the four girls had an unshakeable belief in the quality of their music that wasn't going to be destroyed by a few knock-backs. Because they were all devoted musicians and had also become best friends, they were able to rely on each other for support and wait for the right opportunity.

Then finally they struck gold. Manager John

Benson happened to be friends with Tracy Bennett (he's a bloke!), the big cheese at London Records, formerly home of original eighties' girl band Bananarama and, more recently, East 17. He asked Tracy to listen to a tape of the girls' songs. Bennett admits he was reluctant to listen to it at first. 'But when I put it on, I realized he had brought me the best demo in the whole world. There were six songs on there and they were all hits. By the time the tape had reached the first chorus in "Never Ever", I was getting everyone into my office to listen. I couldn't believe my luck. I've dealt with a lot of bands, but Shaznay is the best songwriter I've worked with.'

London Records publicist, Mel Thomas, was equally impressed. 'When we first heard their demo we thought it was so good there had to be a catch,' she says, 'like they looked really terrible. But they turned out to be gorgeous and we were, like, we've got to sign them.'

And so they did, in November 1996. 'It was amazing! And a real relief as well,' shouts Mel. 'We had a meeting with Tracy Bennett one Tuesday,' recalls Shaz, 'and by the next Tuesday we were in a studio doing our first photoshoot.'

London Records was so confident that All Saints would soon be topping the charts that it spent

£200,000 on TV advertising for their album. And before their first single was released, Bennett predicted, 'All Saints are going to be one of the biggest bands in the world.' How right he was.

Benson started making a video charting the girls' rise to fame. He wasn't just being sentimental – he was a businessman and he knew that not only were All Saints a great proposition, but the video would be in years to come as well. Let's hope they release it soon!

And while the advent of the Spice Girls had created a few problems for All Saints, the 'other girl group,' as Mel now calls them, also opened doors for them by showing everyone that girl bands could become massively successful. Suddenly there were all-female groups everywhere – Cleopatra, Vanilla, Fab!, T-Shirt, B★Witched – but Shaz, Mel, Nic and Nat were light years ahead of the others.

London Records had wanted All Saints to build slowly on their success so that they would retain their credibility, like Eternal. But it was out of their hands. The public were lapping up anything remotely Saintly. Their first single, 'I Know Where It's At', which had been written an incredible four years previously, was finally released on 18 August 1997 and went straight in at number four in early

September. 'It's amazing to think there are so many people out there who like what we're doing,' said Shaz, in a serious state of shock. It stayed in the charts for eight weeks.

Soon it became impossible to get away from All Saints. After playing all over Britain on the Radio 1 roadshow, they then wowed the producers of Channel 4's *The Big Breakfast* by singing 'I Know Where It's At' live – and got themselves the job of being guest presenters for a week. Then they performed on the National Lottery show and at the MTV awards before winning over armies of European fans with a promotional tour of Germany and appearing in Holland at the 1997 Pepsi Pop festival.

But it was the *Smash Hits* tour in November that really gave the girls a taste of the adoration that was to come. Headlining with top acts like Kavana, 911, Ant & Dec and Peter Andre, the enthusiastic reception they got couldn't have been more different from the last time Mel and Shaz had appeared. Just two weeks after releasing that first single, they were voted number two in *Smash Hits'* Best Newcomers poll and number five in the Best Band poll.

All Saints were on a roll and capitalized on their

new-found fame by releasing their second single, 'Never Ever'. A classic pop record, it couldn't have been more different from the up-tempo 'I Know . . .', and demonstrated the girls' immense range, while drawing in even more fans by appealing to an older audience. The song finally reached the top spot on 11 January 1998, shifting a double platinum 1.2 million copies in all in the UK. That same week, the album, also called *All Saints*, which they had released on 24 November, peaked at number two in the charts. To date, it has gone treble platinum and has sold over one million copies in Britain alone.

All Saints' third single, the double A-side 'Under the Bridge' and 'Lady Marmalade' was backed up by what the press were calling a 'mini movie'. This included videos for both singles and cost a whopping £500,000 to make. The nine-minute film took four months to shoot, and was shown at 400 cinemas across Europe just before screenings of the hit movie *Jackie Brown*. All proceeds were to go to breast cancer charities. The video was breathtaking, but then that was hardly surprising – the special effects had been done by the experts that created the *Batman and Robin* film. The girls did all their own stunts, and Nat was lucky to escape unhurt when she was knocked over by an explosion on the set.

Another big bang happened a few weeks later – when their single exploded into the charts, going straight in at number one on 3 May. And despite being knocked off its pedestal the following week by Aqua's 'Turn Back Time', All Saints proved their staying power by fighting back to reclaim the top slot seven days later.

Bennett's prediction had come true – All Saints really were one of the biggest bands in the world. All that hard work had finally paid off. 'I'm glad we went through everything,' says Shaz. 'There's nothing I regret, because if we hadn't gone through it all, we may not have woken up and known what we know now. It's fate – everything happens for a reason.'

CHAPTER FOUR

Tricky Nicky

FACT FILE
Birthday: 7 December 1974
Nickname: The Fonz or Fonzie
Distinguishing marks: Chinese Year of the Tiger tattoo just below her belly-button ring
Most used phrase: 'Gooonks!' which means a real wally

NIC TRIVIA
- She saved an otter from drowning.
- Her false eyelash once came off on stage.
- She and Mel tried to stay up all night in New York by drinking coffee and Diet Coke – but they just ended up feeling sick!
- She hates it when water gets stuck in her ear after being in the shower.

- Her lucky number is seven because that's the date she was born on.

Stunning blonde, brown-eyed Nicole Marie Appleton came strutting into all our lives playing the supermodel in the 'I Know Where It's At' video and, after that entrance, there was no turning back. The most outgoing and bubbly of the band, Nic has won over countless male fans and is many people's favourite All Saint. A poll on one of around fifty websites on the Internet dedicated to the girls has Nic out in front with thirty-four per cent of the votes (closely followed by her older sister Nat).

But it wasn't always like this – Nic says that at school she was a real nerd. 'I had grim, greasy hair and rat tails. All my clothes were hand-me-downs. I spent most of my childhood out of fashion.' That's how she got her nickname – the Fonz (after the cool dude in the TV comedy *Happy Days*). 'Mel invented it to boost my credibility.' That's what friends are for!

The Appleton sisters had an exciting transatlantic upbringing. They were born in Canada to British parents, and Nic had an early taste of fame at school there as a cheerleader for the football team. 'I was on the front of our school magazine in my outfit,' she says proudly. Sadly, the girls' parents divorced when Nic was nine and their Jewish mother brought the whole family (including older sisters Lori and Lee) to London in 1983, where they enrolled in drama school. Fortunately for All Saints this happened to be the same school that Mel went to. Nic and Mel soon found they had a lot in common – including a wild streak that sometimes got them into trouble – and they went on to become great friends.

Then the Appletons' mum met an American and the family moved to New York. For Nic this was especially tough because she desperately missed her new best friend. Nat says that all she could talk about was 'Mel this, Mel that.' But moving around so much did mean that the family became very close. 'We went to about a hundred schools,' says Nat. 'We're like bookends. We're inseparable.'

After she left school, Nic tried a variety of jobs with a spectacular lack of success. She was sacked from every job she ever did – from waitress, bartender and lifeguard to babysitter. 'The most embarrassing time was as an ice-cream vendor in NY. I bent down to tie my shoelace and a big umbrella crashed on to my head. Over ninety dollars' worth of ice cream was stolen while I was out cold.'

Cheeky Nic brings out the fun-loving side of All Saints. She describes herself as 'sweet, easy-going and totally mad. I'm the life and soul of the group. When they're in a bad mood I liven them up.' And when you've got such a mountain of work on your shoulders it really helps to have someone around who's always laughing and joking to keep your spirits up. There's certainly never a dull moment when Nic's around – she can hardly keep her mouth shut. She likes to natter so much that she carries two mobile phones with her at the same time and is always gossiping to someone. 'I'm a really nosy person and like to know everything,' she admits.

Nic has always been known for her mischievous streak and was well-known at school for making up stories. When she was much younger, she once told her friends that she would show them her pet wolves if they gave her some chocolate. The wolves didn't exist, but Nic ended up with a huge stash of choccies!

Nic's also quite argumentative and always tries to get her own way. This can lead to blazing rows, especially with her sister. 'I like getting everything off my chest,' says Nic. 'But if I start rowing with my male friends they'll say, "Oooh look at you trying to be Miss Bossy Boots all of a sudden." Sometimes I need to be put in my place.'

As much as Nic likes going out partying and being outrageous, she's also very homely. She loves to relax with a video of a gangster film (her dream date is Robert De Niro) or a musical like *Grease*. But, in contrast to her sister, she'd rather hide behind the couch than watch something scary – she can't even bring herself to watch *Crimewatch*!

Nic loves reading interviews and articles about All Saints and used to keep a diary charting everything that was happening to them but now she's too busy. She carries a Walkman with her everywhere though, to keep up on the latest music.

Nic lives on her own in a studio flat in London's Belsize Park, a few streets away from Nat and her parents and two minutes walk from Noel of Oasis. Nic doesn't get lonely though – she's got her cats, Nathan and Nathana, to keep her company, who she rescued from a shelter for unwanted pets. 'I'm crazy about them,' says Nic, 'they're more dependable and loving than any man.' When she's away, her mother and older sisters look after them.

'Otherwise they'd be extremely skinny by now,' she jokes.

Her mother can also keep an eye on Nic now – when she first joined All Saints Nic says her mum used to phone her from America all the time to check she was eating properly. No danger of that – Nic loves to pig out on McDonalds, bangers and mash with gravy, Italian food, and between meals she's always stuffing her face with crisps.

When it comes to guys, she's looking for someone who is outgoing and confident, as well as successful and ambitious. Someone who could teach her things but make her laugh at the same time. 'If somebody was to sit down and tell me what they're doing and they were so excited about it, I'd give them my undivided attention,' says Nic. 'I love it when people are enthusiastic about something they love. I don't like guys who'd rather watch TV than have a good chat.'

Nic always seems to fall for guys who are real macho types. Her perfect guy would be a mixture of Liam from Oasis and George Clooney from *ER*, 'with the more serious, romantic, mature side combined with a crazy, living-on-the-edge side.' She admits to fancying actor Christian Slater and Johnny Vaughan from *The Big Breakfast*. Sometimes she's even liked the same guy as sister Nat but she's never made a move.

When Nic was growing up she didn't have much luck with boys. She chucked one guy after she caught him looking at himself in the mirror while she was kissing him and she had a real cringe-worthy experience at school in America. 'The choir would sing Valentine's messages to you from lads,' says Nic. 'I was coming out of the toilet once and there was the whole choir standing there with a card for me from this guy, Robert. And he was soooo ugly. Then they sang this love song to me – it was really embarrassing.'

Then, four years ago, Nat set Nic up on a blind date with the brother of her boyfriend and Nic ended up going out with him for a year. Their mother didn't approve at all and even now she loses her temper if anyone mentions his name. As it turned out she was right – he broke Nic's heart.

But being in All Saints has done wonders for Nic's love life. Before they hit the big time, Nic hadn't had a boyfriend for two years. Then suddenly even people like Kavana were saying that they fancied her. She was also spotted in a club with actor Brad Pitt (who's a friend of their manager) over Christmas 1997. And when she met

Fun Lovin' Criminals lead singer, Huey, at London's trendy Met Bar, he really fell for her and spent the next day ringing record companies trying to get her telephone number. Older sister Nat now describes Nic as 'the boy-mad member of the band' and says that she's always flirting. Nic says she can't help it: 'It's my personality. I'm just nice.'

She didn't hold back on the flirting when she bumped into Robbie Williams while filming *TOTP* on her birthday. She had a huge crush on him but thought she was too big and not pretty enough for him! She couldn't have been more wrong. They started going out together a few weeks later and then, after a whirlwind romance, announced their engagement in June '98. 'He's got his wild side and his sweet, quiet side,' she says, adding that on Valentine's Day he took her out for a romantic meal and bought her 100 red roses. 'He's hit the nail on the head.'

One of the biggest attractions was that their lifestyles were so similar. Apart from anything else they were both in the top ten together for a long time – with 'Never Ever' and 'Angels'. 'It was great,' says Nic. 'We'd both be sitting there on a Sunday, listening to the charts on the radio. I was always ahead of him!'

But then the sensational All Saints have always been ahead of just about everybody. Nic couldn't be happier. 'I just wanted to be the best in whatever I did,' she says. She's certainly achieved that.

STAR QUALITIES

Sagittarians are open, friendly people, as well as being outspoken and hot-headed – they hardly ever think before opening their mouths. If, like Nic, they are born in the Chinese Year of the Tiger, they are true dreamers, always fantasizing about foreign adventures and desert islands and are well-suited to careers which involve travel, such as being in a pop group. However, they miss the people they love and, because they feel uncomfortable with strangers, they can start to misbehave. Even while they are the centre of attention, they are secretly wishing they were somewhere else.

Sagittarian Tigers are inventive, ambitious and hard-working but not in the conventional sense – they don't like to be tied down to the run-of-the-mill routine of a nine-to-five job. They want to get on with their own thing, whatever other people think. Good careers would be acting or fund-raising. In relationships they're not particularly trusting and don't like to be taken for granted.

They need to be constantly reassured that they are loved. Because they are so reluctant to grow up, they may remain single for a long time. Best love matches are Leo, Libra and Aquarius.

CHAPTER FIVE

Nat's Show Business

FACT FILE
Birthday: 14 May 1973
Nicknames: Fat Cat because she was a chubby baby, Nona, Naaatalie
Distinguishing marks: Red Canadian Maple Leaf tattoo on her leg

NAT TRIVIA
- She gets annoyed in clothes shops when someone in front is trying to pay for something really cheap like a pair of tights with a credit card.
- Nat appeared in the TV series *Grange Hill* in 1986 (watch out for reruns).
- Her hair got so dry once from all the styling, she had to slap grease all over it and hide it under a baseball cap for a week.

- She says the best thing that ever happened to her was meeting Snow White and the Seven Dwarfs at Disneyworld.

Not only is Natalie Jane Appleton the older sister of Nic, she's the older sister of the whole band. As she is two years their senior, she tends to fuss and look after the others and often comes across as the leader or spokesperson. She has brought a cool, calm presence to the group, which blends well with Mel and Nic's wild antics and Shaznay's shyness.

But the others sometimes accuse her of being really bossy. Nat says she only interferes because she cares. 'I'm very emotional. I do all the suffering for everybody. I don't sleep at night worrying,' she says in her funny half-English, half-North American accent. When she was younger she was always having rows with Nic because she didn't approve of her boyfriends, but it was only because she couldn't stand to see her little sis get hurt. These days, Nat still takes it out on Nic if she gets annoyed with the band. 'I'm used to getting my own way,' she admits, 'but I can't boss Nic around as much any more. In the band, we respect each other's opinions.' If they do fight, they always make up quickly and five minutes later they'll have forgotten all about it.

Nat's down-to-earth, friendly and outgoing and, even though she's older, can act up as much as the others – as she has done all her life. When she was a kid, Nat cut off almost all of Nic's lovely long hair while their parents were out. Not surprisingly, they went ballistic and poor old Nic had to wear hats for months afterwards. These days, Nat knows that Nic's old enough to get her own back so she plays pranks on other people instead. Once, in America, she pretended to be Madonna and dressed up exactly like the Material Girl and fooled everybody. Now of course, she doesn't need to pretend to be a superstar – she *is* one.

Nat always knew that she wanted to be a singer. When she was a kid, she'd put talcum powder on her face, play air guitar and pretend she was in the heavy metal band Kiss. When she's got time, she plans to learn the guitar for real. She was also the first All Saint to start singing professionally. With the help of her mum, she managed to land a job singing in a New York bar at the age of fifteen. 'I quit school to do that. They never knew how young I was,' says Nat, 'I loved it.' Her ambition is 'to be singing for years to come.'

At school Nat was a fast runner and really good at hockey – although she jokes that her secret was to smash the other girls' ankles. Maybe out of fear for her own shapely legs, she gave it up to do ballet. She took dance exams, then went on to become an aerobics teacher. No wonder she looks so good on stage now!

But all that sport and exercise didn't come easy. She broke her ankle when she was ten and then her nose three years later, for which she had to undergo surgery to make sure it healed properly. The doctor must have been top drawer because there's no way you can tell now.

Nat found herself in hospital again when she had to have her wisdom teeth removed. For most people this would be a nightmare, but Nat loved it. 'I used to look forward to going for a dental check-up because I'd hope he was going to give me a filling. I have loads of them now,' says Nat, insisting that if she wasn't making a mint from singing, she'd have been asking other people to open their mouths. 'I know it sounds odd but I've always wanted to be a dentist.'

Brave Nat doesn't get scared easily and loves reading horror stories by writers such as Stephen King. 'I'll come home at one in the morning and

I've still got to read for half an hour before I go to sleep,' she says. 'I watched horror films from the age of seven. It takes me away from life completely.' She wasn't even frightened when she once thought she saw a ghost on Nic's bed. But there are two things that send a shiver down her spine – spiders and flying. And unfortunately for Nat, since All Saints have become mega she's had to get on a jumbo more and more often.

The only thing that cheers her up on a long plane journey is the in-flight film – Nat loves movies, especially weepy, romantic stories like *Dirty Dancing* (Nic reckons that her older sister always cries at *E.T.*). If she had a choice though, Nat would watch films at home – she doesn't even like the cinema. 'You can't stop the film if you want to go to the toilet,' moans Nat. 'And if you cry you look really stupid.'

About the only chance Nat gets to wind down is at home with her parents in Camden. She'll have a long hot bath, before settling down in front of the telly. She got a bit of a shock recently though, when she saw herself in a repeat of *Grange Hill*. She had a small speaking part in several episodes twelve years ago as one of school bully, Imelda Davis' gang. She dyed her hair especially for the role but it went wrong and ended up going grey. 'It looked horrible,' says Nat.

She loves Italian and Chinese food – but potential boyfriends beware, she won't eat anything unless you've washed your hands first. Oh, and she might belch afterwards – it's one of her bad habits, like not tidying her room and biting her nails. 'They're disgusting. Split, chapped, dry, and flaky – horrendous,' she shudders.

It's hard to believe now, but Nat has had a fair few disasters with boys too. Once she was trying to look cool as she walked past a boy she fancied, but her laces got caught. 'I went flying down the street like Superman. I wanted the ground to swallow me up.' Another time she fell down the stairs while she was trying to impress a boy. And one guy she went out with ended up having a fight in the street because someone said something rude about her. 'My date ended up in hospital. It wasn't very romantic,' she remembers.

'I wasn't the girl all the boys fancied. Not in England anyway,' says Nat. 'But by the time I went to high school in America I started blossoming. I became a cheerleader and then the guys started fancying me.' Nat gained in confidence and started to show off, even dying her hair red once.

Suddenly Nat was the school babe, despite wearing 'men's clothes' like blazers and Levi's. 'I once went out with a guy for just one day,' says Nat. 'He was so cut up he didn't go out with anyone for a year after that.'

But before she got too big for her boots, Mel and Shaz brought her down to earth. They sent her a Valentine's card and Nat thought it was from this really good-looking guy. 'But even though it was all a hoax, it still made me feel special,' she says. Aah.

Nat's ideal man would be Brad Pitt, 'because he's really quiet and down to earth', and she thinks footballers are cute too, especially Ian Wright. She likes dark-haired, well-dressed men who can dance and don't try too hard to impress her, but are just good fun. She likes to have to fight to get her man – not to have someone following her around like a lost puppy. But she's become pretty good at getting what she wants – she's an expert flirt (it must run in the Appleton family). Her hot tip is to smile slowly and flutter her eyelashes. 'You have to be different and original. If you're going somewhere dressy, don't dress up, and if you're going somewhere undressy, dress up,' she advises.

Nat's pretty fussy because she was badly hurt

when she was younger. She got married in America when she was nineteen but sadly it all went horribly wrong. Luckily, one good thing came out of it – her daughter, Rachel, who she adores. So much so that Nat nearly didn't join All Saints because she couldn't bear to be apart from Rachel while the band were out of the country. Fortunately for all of us, her parents stepped in to look after her while Nat's away.

She's now much tougher with boyfriends. 'I'm a heart-breaker,' she says. 'If they're not perfect, forget it.' But then Nat met someone who *was* perfect – *Live & Kicking* and *The O-Zone* presenter Jamie Theakston (who Mel jokingly calls Mr Giraffe). They started going out after Jamie interviewed All Saints on television in October '97 and everyone found out when they turned up at the Brit awards together. In April '98 they jetted off to Venice for a four-day romantic holiday and looked very much in love. 'I've got a soulmate to share things with now and that's great,' said Jamie. 'And I get on brilliantly with her daughter.'

Life couldn't be much better for Nat. Even if things don't work out with Jamie, she's in one of the most popular bands in the world, doing what she's always wanted to do – sing. Not only that, she's doing it with her three best mates. 'Whatever happens,' she says, 'I'll always be behind them and they'll always be behind me. That's a good feeling.'

STAR QUALITIES

Taureans born in the Chinese Year of the Ox are careful, deliberate people, who think everything through extremely thoroughly. They make wise decisions and have the ability to explain things clearly and passionately. No wonder Nat was initially tempted by the idea of becoming All Saints' manager. Their main aim in life is to succeed at whatever they do (they tend to be artistic) and gain fame and respect. They are workaholics, always pushing and striving for the next goal. Attractive and seductive, they also have a great ability to make others feel good about themselves. They adore home comforts and like nothing better than snuggling up in a big comfy armchair with loads of cushions. Taurean Oxes are confident in their own abilities and have very firm views which they refuse to change even under fierce criticism. In family matters they can be a little overbearing and demanding (this explains why Nat is always trying to interfere in Nic's love life). They are suited to jobs where hard work really pays off, such as an

A girly get-together at one of many award ceremonies.

Sitting pretty – the Saints get comfy.

The Saints stun the audience with their live performance at the 1998 Brit Awards.

It's tears all round as the girls receive their **Brit Awards** (and thank their mums).

Nat – going for the dramatic look.

Shaznay – getting the crowd going.

Mel – she's got the funk.

Nic – singing her heart out.

athlete, journalist or researcher. In relationships they can be cruel if they feel they are not being treated properly but are normally extremely caring. They need partners who will be patient and allow them to blossom in their own time. Ideal love matches are Pisces, Cancer, Capricorn and Virgo.

CHAPTER SIX

Simply Shaz

FACT FILE

Birthday:	14 October 1975
Nicknames:	Bart (because she raps like Simpson junior), T, Banana-man
Distinguishing marks:	Year of the Rabbit tattoo on her chest, birthmark on her right hand
Most used phrases:	'For real', 'Can you cope?' and 'No way' ('But not "no way no way no way"', she says, careful to avoid comparisons with Vanilla)

SHAZ TRIVIA
- She loves to thrash people at badminton.
- She once dyed her hair blonde and hated it.

- Shaz hates cooking but has a sweet tooth and loves Twix bars.
- When she found out she'd passed her driving test, she kissed her examiner.
- She saved a man's life after he collapsed in Oxford Street by stopping his bleeding with a pile of tissues before the ambulance turned up.

Forget all the showbiz glamour and celebrity boyfriends. There is no doubt who is the most important person in Tricia Shaznay Lewis' life – her mum. 'Music isn't more important to me than my family,' the half-Jamaican, half-Barbadian insists.

Her mum emigrated to England from the West Indies and had to sweat it out as a dinner lady to support the family – that's Shaz and her sister, Elaine, who is eleven years older. Shaz was born in Islington in London and has lived there with her mum all her life. Their relationship is especially close as her father left them when Shaznay was just a kid. 'She put up with me bumming around, borrowing money when I was doing my music and now for the first time in my life I can give her money,' says Shaz, adding that her ambition is 'to do everything I want in life and make mum proud.'

Shaz describes herself as 'quiet, shy, genuine and a deep thinker' and despite being the driving force behind the band, she is surprisingly modest in interviews, mumbling barely audible answers if she speaks at all. 'I don't want people to get the wrong impression. When they respect us for the music I'll start messing around and having a laugh.'

While Shaz comes across as sensitive and sensible, she has got a fun, crazy side to her – and she isn't afraid to speak her mind. She recently lost her temper in an interview when being asked about the Spice Girls (yet again), and she's not afraid of naming people she doesn't like – which includes the self-styled hard man of rock, Liam from Oasis. 'Shaznay's a Jekyll–and–Hyde character,' says Nic.

When she's got some time off, she'll hang out with her best friend, Rochelle, who lives next door, or curl up on the sofa to watch soaps like *EastEnders*, *Hollyoaks* or *Brookside* (Sinbad is her favourite character) and chat shows like *Ricki Lake*. She says the thing she hates most in the world is 'losing the remote control'. Her favourite film is *Dumb and Dumber*, but that's no reflection on Shaz's own mental abilities – she's got five GCSEs in photography, media studies, English, music and art, and she can even speak Japanese.

When she was sixteen, her dentist told her she needed braces because she used to suck her thumb when she was younger, but she refused because she thought that it would put boys off. Eventually her sensible side won out and she joined Ike Hanson as being one of a tiny group of people ever to wear braces while having a number-one record. She now has perfect teeth after removing the braces in February. She describes herself as 'the same as Naomi Campbell but shorter,' and thinks her back is the favourite part of her body, but potential boyfriends should be wary about the other bits: 'I can't stand my belly button being touched. It freaks me out,' she says.

Despite being terrified by spiders and moths, Shaznay's brave when it comes to other scary stuff. 'I used to play with a ghost when I was about six. He was a rockabilly and had greased-back hair like Elvis. My mum says I was talking to nothing.' Maybe he gave her some top music tips – her inspiration clearly didn't come from her parents. 'They're not musical at all, unless you count my mum singing round the house all the time. My dad wants me to get a proper job. But I don't know how to do anything else.'

Shaz did try other careers, but nothing clicked.

She was a gardener, a postwoman and, at one time, seriously thought about becoming a policewoman. She even played football for Arsenal Ladies, but would miss the practices and just turn up for the matches. 'And if I didn't score loads of goals, I'd get really upset and quit!' she laughs.

But after all the hard work and setbacks, everything came good for Shaz when All Saints won those two Brit awards. That's why the tears came flooding. 'It was overwhelming,' she says. 'I remember thinking, "God I wish I'd written something down..." I'm so embarrassed. My mum made me watch it the next day, and guess what? I cried again because I felt really sorry for myself.'

'Everyone else felt sorry for you too,' interrupts Mel.

'Moments like those are the only time our success feels real,' adds Shaz. 'Most of the time what is happening to the band doesn't affect me. I'm usually too busy to notice.'

When it comes to her love life, Shaz's been positively Saintly compared to the others. Despite the fact that the other three say she's the sexiest Saint, she has only dated three guys in her life. One of those was mechanic Michael Miller, who inspired the lyrics for 'Never Ever'. 'Love's the nicest thing in the world – but also the most dangerous,' warns Shaz.

She's put off by indecisive men, and goes for caring, thoughtful, romantic types who like to cuddle, ideally someone tall and well-scrubbed. She likes quiet blokes, although she admitted in the past that her ideal man was Robbie Williams. Apparently, she was hoping to meet him when All Saints played the Concert of Hope in December '97 for the Princess Diana Memorial Fund. 'I've been quoted saying I want him to ask me out. But he hasn't called. I guess he's too busy.' In the end of course it was Nic who ended up going out with Robbie, but it hasn't affected their friendship.

The youngest All Saint has been linked with Matt Goss from eighties' boy band Bros, and Wayna from Boyz II Men, but she insists they're both 'just good friends'. However, Shaz did admit in April that there was a new love in her life, rumoured to be Damon from Blur. She won't reveal her new guy's identity, however. 'It's a secret,' insists Shaz. 'But he's got a great personality. My way of getting close is by teasing him the whole night, so I never compliment him that much. But I should do because he's gorgeous.' She also says she would never cheat on a guy – so whoever he is, he's a lucky bloke. One thing's for sure, it's not Peter Andre – she says if he ever asked her for a date she'd definitely be washing her hair!

Shaz still can't believe that people are singing along to the songs that she wrote in her bedroom. She is just a normal girl trying to lead a normal life – but when you're mega-famous it's not easy. She'll go shopping, dancing or work out. But even then she can't escape and hates being recognized. 'I went to the gym and our video came up on the screen. I was so embarrassed.' Shaz doesn't like being under the spotlight and says that the more famous she gets, the more likely it is she'll become a hermit. 'I've never been one of those people who's always thought, "I'm going to be famous." I just think of my life as doing music, getting into a studio, releasing a record and that is it.' Let's hope she keeps doing it well into the next millennium.

STAR QUALITIES

Librans are extremely cautious, weighing up all the options before making a decision. But if they are born in Chinese Rabbit years, like Shaz, they are even more reluctant to commit themselves and find it difficult to trust people. They are very suspicious and often end up holing up in the safety of their homes, which will be the ultimate in cosiness and comfort. Because they hate to fight and don't like being told what to do, Libran Rabbits are best suited to careers in which they have a lot of freedom to do what they want – such as music, writing or interior decorating. Libran Rabbits prefer to remain behind the scenes and let someone else do the talking (and in the case of All Saints, Shaz has three band members only too willing to do just that). They come across as calm, sensible and graceful and when they do go out they make an effort to entertain and be the centre of attention. After meeting them just once, you will never forget them. They see beauty everywhere, are generous and passionate and regularly fall in love, but will rarely commit to a long-term relationship and struggle to find anyone who comes up to their high standards. If a guy is interested in Shaz, he must try to keep his distance a bit and keep her guessing. Best love matches are Gemini, Leo, Sagittarius and Aquarius.

CHAPTER SEVEN

Heaven and Mel

FACT FILE
Birthday: 25 March 1975
Nicknames: Smell-anie, Blatt Fink, Mel-odie. 'Shaznay calls me Smell. Nic and Nat call me Bucket.'
Distinguishing marks: Navy Chinese-style dragon on her left rib cage and musical notes on her right shoulder, two-foot scar on her back from her neck to her trousers
Most used phrases: 'No mate' and 'Blatantly'

MEL TRIVIA
- She sang on a band called Dreadzone's first album and appeared on TV with them as their

backing singer – along with Denise Van Outen.
- Her favourite drink is milk.
- Eyelash curlers are the one thing Mel can't live without.
- She fancies Sean Connery.
- Mel can touch her nose with her tongue.

Mel may be the shortest Saint, but she's also the loudest. You can always rely on Melanie R. Blatt to shoot her mouth off. 'I'm the cynical one of the group ... of the world, probably,' she says. Fiery Mel's got an opinion on everything and she's not afraid to share it. Mel herself thinks her dragon tattoo sums up her character. 'I'm pretty shy underneath and the dragon represents power and fierceness.'

Take, for instance, her now famous Spice Girls quote: 'We're much better looking and we've more upstairs.' And despite sharing a name with a Spice Girl – Mel B – and going to school with Baby Spice ('I knew her to say hello and we spent some lunchtimes together'), she just can't help herself.

Another band to cross Mel's firing line was Aqua. 'At least we're not thirty and singing about Barbie,' she said.

She's definitely getting herself a reputation as the really mouthy one of the four – and not without due cause. 'I'll argue with anyone,' she says. 'I love seeing how far I can push people. People always look at me as if to say, "You're a nutter."'

She wasn't always so crazy though. Mel used to be a lot less confident and would cry herself to sleep when things weren't going right. 'But being in this business has made me strong and I'm proud that I haven't cried for over a year,' she says.

Mel had an unconventional childhood by any stretch of the imagination. Her French mum and English dad were hippies and named her after a 1960's singer. Little did they know that Melanie would end up doing the same thing. But they did get her started on music early – they took her to Glastonbury rock festival when she was six and 'made me stand on the roof of the car and play the viola.'

Her parents ran their own business designing T-shirts for heavy metal band Metallica and she spent her early years growing up on a houseboat in London's King's Cross. Later on she even lived in a warehouse. 'We didn't have anywhere to live, so we all ended up in their T-shirt factory. I thought it was great,' laughs Mel. Her parents also had an astrological chart done for their daughter which said she'd be successful and sorted by the time she was twenty-five. It looks like being pretty much on the ball.

Mel went to drama school aged eleven and was a star pupil. She recorded a toothpaste ad with Emma Spice and acted in the West End musical *Les Miserables*. But disaster struck when she was aged thirteen. One of Mel's teachers noticed that she was having difficulty dancing and the doctor told her she had scoliosis (a curved spine). Mel's dream of becoming a ballet dancer was in tatters. Worse still, she was advised to have a major operation – with no guarantee of a complete cure. 'The health service said the operation had a fifty per cent chance of leaving me paralysed,' says Mel. 'My mother said, "That's it – we're out of this country."'

And so the Blatts moved across the Channel and Mel underwent surgery the following year in France. She had a metal rod inserted in her back with three hooks clipping her spine together. 'It hurt,' admits Mel, although now she forgets it's there, which has caused a bit of bother travelling round the world with All Saints. 'I set off alarms at airports,' she laughs.

At least her back was cured. 'It means I can't do the crab, that's all,' she says, bravely. 'Dealing with it has made me stronger.'

Living in France was a culture shock for Mel. 'I'd lived in London all my life and suddenly found myself in a small village full of old men and I couldn't speak a word of French.' However, the family returned to England when Mel was sixteen. Her boyfriend was supposed to be coming too, but he never turned up. 'I went back three months later and he was going out with some other girl called Melanie,' she says. He must be kicking himself now.

Mel took her mind off things by doing a variety of jobs to make ends meet. She was a nanny, a window dresser and a shop assistant in trendy store Kookaï, although that lasted just three hours! She started at ten a.m. and walked out at one p.m. Luckily for us, Mel stuck at her musical career a little longer.

The All Saint with the biggest lips is actually a bit of a slob. She hates exercise and says that if she could be an animal she would be a tortoise because they just laze around all day. She chills by chatting with friends or watching romantic movies like *Gone with the Wind*. On TV she loves *EastEnders* ('It reminds me of my childhood'), *Friends*, *The Simpsons* and *Shooting Stars*. One of the best presents she ever had was when Nic took her to see *Ready, Steady, Cook* being filmed because she's a dab hand in the kitchen. 'I can cook anything,' she says. 'That's the French side of me. I make a mean cheese fondue. Unfortunately it doesn't agree with Shaz's stomach – but she liked it before she vomited.'

Mel loves food so much she'll eat anything and pigs out on peanut-butter sandwiches, spaghetti, McDonalds and 'anything with butter, cream and cheese or just fat.' It's a wonder how she manages to stay so gorgeous. Maybe all that partying keeps her fit.

Once Mel got into trouble when she threw a bash at her parents' house while they were away. She thought she'd made extra sure they wouldn't find out by cleaning up everything, but she didn't look outside – there was a pile of sick on the doorstep. Perhaps she'd been cooking fondue again!

She also got into hot water with her mum when she had her first tattoo done – the musical notes. Mel's not too pleased with it herself now 'because there's only five staves on a music score, and he's put in six.' For one of the most famous singers in the world, it's a tad embarrassing.

Mel describes herself as 'calm, jokey and very generous,' and her ambition is to be happy. One of her most memorable moments was watching her younger sister being born and Mel was given the honour of choosing a name for her – Jasmine. These days they get on really well and she even shares a bedroom with the eleven-year-old in their parents' house in Ladbroke Grove, London, where the walls are covered with posters of Hanson and Barbie. The rest of All Saints reckon that Mel is handy to have around. 'She always has whatever you need in her bag,' says Nic. 'Aspirin, Elastoplast, chewing gum. She's the organizer. She's great at sorting out problems, but she's also a bit of a nutter.'

Considering her lovely deep-brown eyes and to-die-for looks, it comes as a bit of a shock that until recently, Mel didn't have much luck with boys. 'I'm not very good at flirting. Nicky has to give me lessons,' says Mel. 'I don't notice when men are coming on to me.'

Only once did Mel do the hard part and chat up a guy at a party – but when it came to the exchanging telephone numbers bit, she got so embarrassed that she avoided him for the rest of the night!

Mel likes well-dressed blokes who make her laugh and can teach her things. Her perfect place for a date is a restaurant, gassing over a candlelit dinner, but unlike Shaz she doesn't like her men to be too caring – she wants someone with so much going on in their life that they don't have time to follow her around. Anyone totally the opposite of Dean Gaffney (Robbie) from *EastEnders*, basically.

But for a long while, Mel wasn't having much luck finding her dream guy, mainly because she was spending so much time with her nose to the grindstone. 'The music's been taking up most of our time,' she said. There were stories about her dating Brad Pitt, and she had admitted that she fancied him in the past, but Mel insists they were just friends. Things got so bad that when she saw Jamiroquai's Jay Kay in the street she jumped on him. 'I said, "I love you." And he said, "Well, we'll be getting married next then,"' she says excitedly.

As fate would have it, Mel ended up with Jamiroquai's bass player instead, Stuart Zender, who she met in January 1997. They fell head over heels in love and Stuart, who's the same age as Mel, bought her a £20,000 engagement ring two months later. 'I love him and every day he does cool things,' says the sultry Saint.

'Mel and I are perfect for each other,' adds millionaire Stuart. 'I have no worries for the future.

Rumours of us splitting up or leaving our groups are wrong.' Phew!

Yes, if Mel's got anything to do with it, All Saints are going to be around for a very long time. 'The music is very important to us,' says Mel. 'We put our heart and soul into it and really love what we do.' She does have something to fall back on, though, just in case. 'If it doesn't work out, I'll go back to playing the flute at Glastonbury.'

STAR QUALITIES

Aries born in the Chinese Year of the Rabbit are refined and cultured, and adore beauty. Mel's love of cooking reflects her desire to create a masterpiece and whatever she makes, it will always be well presented. Aries Rabbits are highly curious and want to get as much out of life as possible. They love to learn and will work their fingers to the bone to achieve their goal, but they don't worry about recognition from others. Good careers would be as a museum curator or restaurant critic. Aries Rabbits love comfort and home security and are sensible and careful, although they will play up from time to time, and all their common sense goes out the window when they go shopping. They are extremely caring but at the same time distant and cool. They are charming and sensitive but prefer to be independent in relationships and don't like partners who are too clingy. They dream of romance and knights in shining armour and are constantly falling in love, but tend to run out at the first sign of trouble. Best love matches are Leo, Sagittarius, Gemini and Aquarius.

CHAPTER EIGHT

Songs in the Key of Life

In the rush to follow in the Spice Girls' footsteps, All Saints left all the other girl bands quaking in their wake. Soon, they'll be bigger than the Spices themselves. Why? Simple. The sheer quality of their music. The girls have succeeded because they are first and foremost great musicians. They received the ultimate accolade in the music industry bible, *Music Week*, which wrote: 'The key thing about one of the best pop albums of the year is the songwriting.' Lucky for us, that should mean that All Saints will be around for a long, long time.

'They are real music fans, obsessives,' says their record company boss, Tracy Bennett. 'They can give you the bar codes on their record collection.' Those collections are extensive. Mel's into R & B, Stevie Wonder, Prince, hip hop and garage (basically 'anything with a good bass line') and says that she started singing after seeing Julie Andrews in the *Sound of Music*. Nic namechecks Oasis, The Prodigy and Robbie Williams, while Nat listens to American rock like REM and old-school rap. But it's the mega-talented Shaz who has the biggest influence on All Saints' unique sound, as she writes ninety per cent of the lyrics and arrangements (she is credited on all but three of the album tracks). Her personal record stash is packed with American rap and hip hop, artists such as Missy 'Misdemeanour' Elliot and Busta Rhymes. 'I love the rhythm, the beat, the poetry, the rhyming,' says Shaz. 'The fact that rap songs are stories and tell the truth. That's where I get a lot of my inspiration, even when I started writing poetry back in school. And that's what led, naturally, to the songwriting.'

There is a great deal of variety on All Saints' album and reviewers have noted a range of influences – from Motown, soul, disco, hip hop, R & B to pop. 'My aim was to appeal to all sorts of people into every type of music,' explains Shaz. 'I wanted indie, teen pop, adult rock, hip hop, soul and R & B fans to like it. I dig all those different sounds, so I didn't want to exclude anyone.'

'We're not in one specific category,' adds Mel.

'Can't say it's hip hop. Can't say it's pop. Can't say it's soul. It's not dance, so what is it?' Who cares how you describe it when it's this good?

The girls' diversity shows itself in their choice of single releases. Their first single 'I Know Where It's At' was an invitation to party – funky singalong pop that gave the perfect first glimpse of a new band poised to take over the world. 'It's an in-yer-face introduction to who we are – no flying penguins or anything fancy,' says Nat. But then they slowed the pace right down with the sublime 'Never Ever', which stamped on the feet of the doubting Thomases who said that the band were one-hit wonders and showcased Shaz's exceptional songwriting talent. 'I just look at life and see it as it is,' she says simply. 'I wrote "Never Ever" four years ago after I split up with the first man I'd ever been in love with. When it all went wrong I was in such pain.'

Of course, 'Never Ever' would go on to give the girls their first number one and two Brit awards, as well as propelling them to superstardom. 'It's funny how something good can come out of such a bad situation,' says Shaz. '"Never Ever" showed itself to be a great track that grew on people gradually. I watched our audience change from week to week

– we began to get more adult fans. Personally, I'm into hard rap, but I know not everyone digs that. I really respect bands like Ocean Colour Scene because they managed to attract me to their songs even though I rarely listen to rock. That's what I wanted us to do too.' They certainly did. Oh, and in case you're wondering, Shaz never did get the letter of explanation she asks for from her boyfriend in the opening rap.

It was Nat's love of American rock that led to the cover of Red Hot Chili Peppers' 'Under the Bridge', which had reached number thirteen for them in 1994. 'I asked our producer if he could come up with a backing track with guitars on it,' she says. 'He brought in a sample from "Under the Bridge" and we couldn't come up with anything, so we covered it, but changed the melody and gave it an All Saints' vibe.' The girls hope that the Chili Peppers like what they've done. 'I'm scared,' shrieks Nic. 'They have long hair and tattoos! They'll jump on us and squash us!'

On the flip side of 'Under the Bridge' is the second cover version from the album, 'Lady Marmalade', which was a chart-topper in 1975 for US soul trio LaBelle.

The one track on the album that all four girls

contributed to is 'Heaven' (in more than just its title). Written in the studio, each Saint came up with a verse about waiting at the pearly gates. 'It's a lot harder to collaborate on songs because there are four very strong minds in the band,' explains Shaz. 'It worked, but it was the hardest thing we had to do.'

They also had trouble with 'Let's Get Started', but for different reasons. In January 1998, All Saints had to pay legal costs after the song was credited to Shaz and producer Johnny Douglas by mistake. They also had to change the name to 'If You Want to Party (I Found Lovin')' on future pressings of the album because it was so similar to the Fatback Band's 1980 disco hit. 'We used a sample which we cleared, but the lyric and arrangement are ours,' says Shaz defensively. 'We made it sound better than the original.' If your copy of the LP has got 'Let's Get Started' on it think yourself lucky. It might be quite rare one day.

All Saints won't have any such problems with the rest of the album as it's all pure Shaznay Lewis. 'War of Nerves' was inspired by Princess Di's accident. 'I never thought about my own death until it happened to Diana,' she says. 'The song helped me face those feelings. Then one fan wrote and said it helped him deal with the death of his mother. That was very touching. If people relate to even one song I wrote, that is the whole deal.'

The girls were helped enormously in writing the music by producer Karl 'K Gee' Gordon, who has stuck by them for years. He is so much part of the team that the girls describe him as the fifth All Saint (you can see how much they appreciate his input in the album thank-you notes). They also enlisted the massive experience of behind-the-scenes geniuses such as Nellee Hooper (who has worked with Björk, Madonna and Janet Jackson), Cameron McVey (Neneh Cherry, Massive Attack) and Johnny Douglas (George Michael) to really polish that All Saints' sound. And for all you trainspotters out there, the album was also co-produced by Magnus Fiennes, younger brother of the actor Ralph, best known for his performance in Oscar-winning film *The English Patient*.

Many of the songs on the album reflect the girls' own experiences, and that includes relationships. '"Get Busy" is about when you've just started dating someone and you're not sure what to do because you don't know what the other person's like,' says Shaz. 'Take the Key' is a straight love song, about how your heart jumps when you see the person of your dreams. And 'Beg' appears on first listen to be another love song, but in reality is the girls' dig at all the people who said they wouldn't make it. On the rest of the album, Shaz really lives up to her Bart nickname on the mega-catchy 'Bootie Call', the girls get down with 'Alone', a bassy rap number and steal your soul with 'Trapped'.

All Saints had pulled off a miracle. They'd made an album that wowed not only teenage fans, but their parents too. Even the critics loved it. Shaz, ever modest, sums up All Saints like this: 'We're not the best singers in the world. We're not Mariah Careys or Whitney Houstons, but we all have unique voices. That's why they work well together.' And there's good news for All Saints' fans everywhere. They're just going to keep churning out more and more great records. As Mel says, 'The day we change our sound is the day we sell our soul.'

CHAPTER NINE

Who Wears the Trousers?

While many female pop groups rely on revealing outfits to attract attention, All Saints know that the quality of their music is enough. They've always refused point blank to be pushed into exposing their bodies – and the only part of an All Saint's body you'll ever see is her tummy!

Nonetheless, they always look sensational in a way that could only be pure All Saints. Their unique style is now an integral part of the band and girls all over the country are copying that street-cool look.

The girls received the ultimate compliment when they were praised by fashion editor Sally Courtis of style bible *Elle*: 'Fashion moves faster than pop. But All Saints is where *Elle* girl is at.

Their look is sexy without being tacky. They are confident, mature and harmonious.'

'We're about being as honest as possible,' explains Mel. 'Nobody tells us how to dress or how to look. I dress the same to go to Sainsbury's as I do when I'm performing.'

'We get asked why we're still in our rehearsal clothes, but that's cool,' continues Nic, who admits that at home they slob around in tracksuits. 'We wear tanks, hooded sweats, painters' pants, hiking boots and snowboard gear that we get in Japan. You won't catch us in tiny skirts. We like to get dressed up, just not very often. We hate being uncomfortable and cold.'

The key items in the All Saints wardrobe are baggy, low-slung combat trousers with ammunition pockets, plain-coloured tight crop T-shirts and Stüssy vests, Tommy Hilfiger hooded tops and jumpers tied round the waist, extra-large black or navy denim jackets, topped off by mammoth quilted coats which reach from head to toe by labels such as Fila or Adidas. Feet are not forgotten either, and are adorned by the latest designer trainers such as Adidas Shell Toes and Nike Silver Gore-Tex, or big clumpy work boots by Caterpillar or Timberland. Designers such as

Kangol, Red Or Dead, Calvin Klein and Donna Karan are firm favourites and the girls shop till they drop in Diesel, Hennes and Top Shop.

Individual touches are important too. Shaz is addicted to trainers, loves Calvin Klein and is rarely seen without her Tommy Hilfiger woolly hat. She is more sensible than the others and loves to bargain-hunt, but complains that these days they don't have time to shop. Nic has mountains of make-up and says her perfect day would have to include clothes shopping with her mates. Mel also loves spending money on clothes and sees no point in hoarding it for a rainy day, admitting, 'I've got my eye on some diamonds in this brilliant jewellery shop I know.' She carries her sunglasses everywhere, owns hundreds of pairs of knickers bought in France or in Marks & Spencer and loves her leather coat. Nat sometimes shares clothes with her sister, but when she goes out with a guy she likes to dress up, often in a leather miniskirt. She's really into designer clothes, like Diesel and DKNY. Like the others, she can't wait to go back to America. 'Everything's so cheap there,' she says, adding that she went mad the last time they were in Chicago. 'I spent every penny I had – about four hundred and fifty pounds.'

The stunning singers can now afford to buy whatever they want. But they are also getting sent mountains of stuff for free by labels hoping that some of the All Saints' cool will rub off on them. Mel says that the best thing about being in All Saints is the free trainers. It's like all their Christmases have come at once!

They've also made friends in very high places. Donatella Versace, head of the trendy Versace empire, is a big fan and flies over designer gear for them from Italy. She also invited the girls to sing live at the launch of her new Versus collection in Milan and afterwards took them into a huge showroom, gave them a dressing room each and told them to take anything they wanted. Shaz chose a trouser suit while Mel took home a gorgeous leather bag worth £2,000.

Now the girls have got all these great clothes, they're determined to look after them. Mel says, 'Donatella gave us all these great, full-length puffa coats. A few days later I saw Björk wearing exactly the same coat but she had lipstick all over one shoulder. It really spoilt the effect, so I'm determined to keep mine clean.'

Shaz doesn't have such worries: 'I'm always buying feather-lined jackets and I don't know how to wash feathers, so I buy a new jacket instead. If I buy one more my mum will go mad.'

It's not always easy being the best-dressed band on the planet. Items such as hipsters can often take on a mind of their own. The girls have never forgotten the time Shaznay's trousers fell down accidentally on the *Smash Hits* roadshow – and we don't suppose the audience have either.

At least experiences like these allow the girls to indulge in their other favourite pastime – buying underwear from Knickerbox and La Senza. 'We've always had a bit of an underwear weakness, but now we have an excuse,' says Nat. 'Everything has to match in case it's seen on stage!'

CHAPTER TEN

Saints in Heaven

All Saints had always believed that their music would conquer the world. But they'd never imagined what would come with it. They hadn't given the notion of fame a second thought. The screaming fans, the endless promotional schedules and interviews with journalist after journalist. But as soon as 'Never Ever' smashed the charts, they weren't to be given a moment's peace.

Soon they were getting recognized wherever they went. 'We were at a garage and these girls shouted out Shaznay's name,' says Nic. 'We all looked because we thought she must know them and they started waving at the rest of us. It was the first time we'd been recognized. It was amazing.'

They couldn't believe it when they were asked to appear on *TOTP* either, because, like most people, it was a show they'd watched all through their childhood, dreaming that one day they might be on it. 'My mum used to say she'd know I had made it when she saw me on *TOTP*,' says Shaz.

Getting to number one was even more breathtaking. Nat was ice-skating when she found out. 'I span around the rink a couple more times and then we all went to Mel's house with all our families,' she remembers. 'Mel's mother made dinner and we celebrated with lots of champagne.' Mel and Shaz say that it was the best moment of their lives.

But the moment it truly dawned on them that all their years of hard work had finally paid off was at the Brits. It was all too much for Shaz and she burst out crying in front of the biggest gathering of pop stars of the year and millions of viewers watching at home. They couldn't have chosen a more public occasion. But it wasn't planned – the girls were genuinely shocked and thrilled and when they got up on that stage in front of all those famous people, all their emotions came flooding out.

Nat admits that it wasn't just Shaz who was blubbing. 'We all had tears in our eyes,' she says. 'We regret it a bit because we didn't want to look like cry babies,' she adds, worried about All Saints' image. 'People might think we're soppy. It makes us worse than Gazza.'

After winning the Brits, All Saints had to get used to the idea of being famous – and fast. Suddenly everyone wanted to meet them and strangers would come up to them in the street. Not only that, everywhere they looked, there were huge photos of them. 'It's weird,' says Nat. 'When I see posters of us, I think, "Who are they?"'

Nic says that they had to start wearing sunglasses and hats just to go shopping. 'I feel like an alien from the planet Uranus,' she adds.

Shaz's personal highlight was when they were invited on to Chris Evans' *TFI Friday* show and comedian Dawn French asked if she could come to their dressing room. 'Dawn French asking us!' screams Shaz. 'She said she and Lenny Henry really loved our music. I wanted to cry.' It seems it was becoming a bit of a habit.

Before they knew it, the girls were travelling the world, meeting loads of cool people and guys like Nick from the Backstreet Boys were saying that he fancied them. Plus, for the first time in years, they had some money in their pockets. And for Mel that meant just one thing – more McDonalds. 'We shouldn't, but we do,' she admits.

Not only was it fun, it was also extremely hard work. They got their first taste of the downside of the pop-star lifestyle when their record company sent them to Japan for a two-week promo trip in the summer of '97. It was a never-ending round of interviews and personal appearances. They even did 127 radio and TV messages in one day! 'They threw us in at the deep end,' says Nic.

'They're workaholics in Japan,' adds Nat. 'The hard-core promotion out there prepared us for promotion here.'

They needed it. The phenomenal success of 'Never Ever' in early '98 catapulted them into orbit. The girls found themselves working from five in the morning until midnight for three months solid. Not only that, they were being whisked from one country to the next before they even had time to look at a map. In March they went over to the States, where 'I Know . . .' was in the top fifty, to meet record company and radio bosses and appear on TV shows such as the famous *Saturday Night Live*, watched by millions of Americans. They were supposed to go straight on to Canada but had an unexpected break in New York when their passports were stolen. 'We wanted to eat at Robert De Niro's restaurant,' says

Nic, 'but the only reservation we could get was too late.'

'We ordered in pizza, watched *Scream* on a huge screen TV and then went to the Backstreet Boys' party in the Rockefeller Center,' adds Mel.

But all too soon it was back to work and they jetted off to Canada, where their album was in the top ten, for yet more meet-and-greets. The girls also performed with a whole host of other bands at an outdoor pop music festival called Snow Job. Also on the bill that day was a local girl group named Dynamiss – starring none other than Nic and Nat's seventeen-year-old cousin, Rena! From Canada they flew via Los Angeles to New Zealand and then Australia before finally coming back to London in April for a well-deserved holiday and the chance to grab some precious time with their boyfriends.

But before they knew it, the rigorous schedule started up again as the girls started filming the video for their fourth single. Then it was a one-off gig for one of the richest men in the world – the Sultan of Brunei. The girls weren't too reluctant about that – he flew them first-class to his palace and reportedly paid them one million pounds for the pleasure. For just one show!

Later in the month the hard work really hit home. They flew to Poland for the weekend and spent two days giving radio and TV interviews for twelve hours before being woken up at the crack of dawn to fly back to London. They got just thirty minutes at home before being launched into more interviews and meetings about mixes for their next single and then being put through a gruelling exercise routine by an ex-army instructor to keep their fitness levels up. The next day they were picked up at six a.m. to fly to Copenhagen and worked until almost midnight when they caught yet another plane to Stockholm. And so it continued.

'We spend most of our time in the air,' jokes Nat. 'We party with the stewards and stewardesses – and we don't forget the pilots.'

'If you get tired, people throw it in your face and say, "Well, this is what you chose to do,"' sighs Mel.

The hard work is paying off. The girls have a growing fan club in all four corners of the world, with devotees as far afield as Sydney, Singapore, Toronto, Kuala Lumpur, Rome, Bangkok and Warsaw. Not forgetting the UK, of course.

'Everywhere we've been has been really cool, but Japan was fantastic,' says Nic. 'It was so different to what I'd expected.' It was certainly the first time the girls had come across fans who would bawl their eyes out as soon as they saw them. Maybe they were impersonating Shaz at the Brits!

'We always get a brilliant reception in Germany,' adds the songwriter supreme. 'Even in countries we've never visited, we've been greeted by loads of fans. In Spain, they love kissing and always give us two pecks.'

'The boys that come up and ask for our autographs are really sweet,' says Nat. 'We've got a lot of girl fans too. They push the guys out of the way. The guys are very shy. It's the girls who've got the guts.'

All Saints' lifestyle sounds fun and glamorous, but there's a down side to the high life. They all say that the worst thing about being famous is travelling and that they miss their families and boyfriends. They'll run up £200-a-day bills on their mobiles talking to their sweethearts (especially Nic). Sometimes, says Mel, 'they can throw me in the baggage hold for all I care. Just get me home.'

'I've never been happier . . . or more tired,' adds Nat. 'We get to the point where we're so tired we get the shakes, but we're learning to relax.'

But it's hard to relax when you can't even walk down the street without being mobbed by adoring fans. 'I always used to wonder why people wore sunglasses inside,' says Mel. 'Now I know why. We're wearing them.'

Shaz still wanders down All Saints Road whenever she has time, no doubt reliving fond memories, but now she worries about how she looks. Nat says that she gets people shouting and looking at her and some even sing outside her front door! She's tried everything to prevent being recognized but it's still no use.

'I was in the airport,' she says, 'and I had a hat on and my big Parka coat up to my nose and this guy came up to me and said, "Nice disguise."'

'Maybe if we dressed like fairies, or in high heels, people wouldn't recognize us,' jokes Nic, although the chances of the coolest, streetest band in the world doing that are smaller than Five getting a sixth member.

The biggest problem for the girls is trying to have a normal relationship with their boyfriends. Wherever they go, they're followed by photographers and piles of stories are written about them that just aren't true. Shaz, as always, is worried about what her mum might think.

Whenever she's seen out with a boy, the papers say that he's her boyfriend. She doesn't even go to hip hop or soul clubs any more because everyone stares at her.

After All Saints appeared on TV for the first time on the National Lottery, Shaz's mum told her that all the neighbours came out on to the street and started pointing at her bedroom window, saying, 'That's where she sleeps.' And since Nat's become famous, she's started to hear from distant family relatives that she's never even met before.

Everywhere they go, the girls have screaming fans and strangers telling them that they love them. It's nice to get home and escape from it all – but even that can be a shock to the system. 'It's really hard when you're home just for one day, and your mum tells you to do the washing-up,' admits Shaz.

'We're not living in reality at the moment,' adds Mel. 'Living off room service and having people do stuff for you all the time, that's not reality. I went on holiday with Stuart, who is also used to travelling everywhere with a tour manager, and we were both like, "We have to check-in ourselves?"'

The stressful lifestyle can lead to arguments. 'We row all the time over the smallest things,' admits Nic. 'It can be nuclear war. But that's why it was so important we weren't manufactured. You have to be close to spend every waking moment together.' Little bust-ups are just a way of letting off steam when the pressure gets too much. In reality all that time spent in each other's pockets has actually brought them closer. Even when they're not working, they'll hang out together (their favourite London haunts are the Met Bar, Atlantic Bar, Momo and Browns). They're just like any other girl gang, sharing in-jokes and gossiping. They've even made up their own language. 'We say "Det" all the time,' explains Nat. 'If we see a good-looking bloke we say he's "Det", which means he's gorgeous.'

It's when they're bored that you've really got to watch out for All Saints. They can get up to all kinds of tricks — in fact, if you had to think up a name for them now, All Saints would probably be bottom of the list. 'We have someone working for us called Richie,' says Nic. 'It was his first day and we had a deadline and he was told to really look after us. So me and Mel decided to run away. We were watching from behind bins and he looked like he was going to freak out.

'Then we got these magazines with all these fake tattoos that don't come off for a week. They had big ones that said, "Girl Power!" He was asleep, so me and Mel licked the tattoos and slapped them on his neck and arms. He was stuck there with this big Girl Power sign across his throat trying to be normal.'

'We try our hardest to make other people blush,' admits Mel.

So are the girls Saints or sinners? 'We sing in a saintly way. It's in between. We're not Saints and we're not sinners. I wouldn't go as far as running away to a convent. There are no boys there,' explains Nic.

All Saints are just a bunch of girls trying to lead a normal life. They're down to earth, like to have a laugh and are genuinely overwhelmed by all the fuss that is being made about them. All they really want to do is make music.

'At the moment we're not singing much – which is what we love doing,' says Shaz. 'All we seem to do is travel from country to country and do a lot of talking. I don't dig that part. It's not about money or fame – if you're not enjoying the music, there's nothing that can make up for that.'

CHAPTER ELEVEN

What's in Store?

In just twelve months, All Saints shot from nobodies to superstars. Suddenly the question on everybody's lips was not which Spice Girl do you fancy, but which All Saint? They had made more money than they could have possibly dreamt of, were adored by male and female fans the world over and, most importantly for the girls, their music was being heard and loved by millions.

They could also count a fair few world leaders in their fan club after singing The Beatles' 'All You Need is Love' at the G8 Summit Concert in Birmingham on 8 May 1998, for the planet's top political figures. They even met American president, Bill Clinton. 'He said he really liked my Caterpillar boots,' reveals Nat. A few days later, they were again in the global spotlight, performing

'Lady Marmalade' at the World Music awards in front of the Prince of Monaco.

They were hot property and everyone wanted in. But All Saints really proved where their loyalties lay when they turned down £500,000 to promote Pepsi in March '98. Fizzy drinks just didn't fit with the All Saints' image. 'It was a massive amount of money,' says Shaz, 'but that's not why we're here. We love making music and want it to speak for itself.'

Although Mel jokes, 'I might regret it when I'm sixty-five and I've got to live in a caravan in Bognor.'

She needn't have worried. Just a month later they received an offer they couldn't refuse – a sponsorship deal with Levi's jeans worth £850,000. This was much more up All Saints' road. The girls all wore Levi's anyway and saw it as a cool brand to be associated with. 'They always believed if the right deal came along with the right company they'd go for it,' explains a record-company spokesman.

Not that they needed the cash. Accountants were predicting that their debut album would go on to sell ten million copies, netting the girls £15 million between them. The first thing that family types Mel and Shaz plan to do with their dosh is buy a house for their parents to thank them for all they've put them through.

But it's not just Mr and Mrs Blatt and Mrs Lewis who are reaping the rewards. There's great news for All Saints' fans everywhere – the girls signed a deal in February 1998 to produce a further two albums and they've already started work on their follow up. Considering the depth of Shaz's incredible songwriting talent, every other band in the universe must be wondering whether the number one spot will ever be free again.

Sadly, though, rumours of a *Spiceworld*-type film aren't true. 'What a load of rubbish,' says Shaz. 'Let me tell you right now, we have no plans to make a film.'

Whatever happens, the girls will stick together. Unlike most other groups, there has never been any talk of them splitting up and pursuing solo careers. And seeing as they stood by each other for five years when nothing was going right, they shouldn't have too many problems now that they've turned into an unstoppable hit factory. 'We're probably closer than ever, because only we know what we've gone through,' says Shaz. All for one and one for all!

That ambition and dedication should enable the band to stay on top of the charts for years to come. As manager John Benson says in the album's cover notes, 'All Saints . . . Your talent knows no boundaries and has yet to flower even more than most can imagine.'

The only obstacle to All Saints ruling the planet is their own reluctance to expose those closest to them to the glare of the media spotlight. 'We want to be successful only to the point where we can still be happy,' says Nic. 'You should be as successful as you can be without damaging yourself, your family or the people you love. You should be able to try and live a normal life.'

That's going to be increasingly difficult for these four girls, especially as their popularity's going to soar even further after they set off on a worldwide tour in 1999. 'It'll be amazing because that's what we're all about,' says Shaz. 'We can't wait.' Join the club.

So what's their secret? 'The only advice we could offer anyone about pop stardom,' says Nat, 'would be something as obvious as, y'know, "Be yourself."' Good luck, everyone!